THE ROYAL HORTICULTURAL SOCIETY
PRACTICAL GUIDES

WALLS & FENCES

THE ROYAL HORTICULTURAL SOCIETY
PRACTICAL GUIDES

WALLS &
FENCES

LINDEN HAWTHORNE

DORLING KINDERSLEY
LONDON • NEW YORK • SYDNEY
www.dk.com

A DORLING KINDERSLEY BOOK
www.dk.com

PROJECT EDITOR Irene Lyford
ART EDITOR Murdo Culver

SERIES EDITOR Gillian Roberts
SERIES ART EDITOR Stephen Josland

SENIOR MANAGING EDITOR Mary-Clare Jerram
MANAGING ART EDITOR Lee Griffiths

DTP DESIGNER Louise Paddick

PRODUCTION Mandy Inness

First published in Great Britain in 2000
by Dorling Kindersley Limited,
9 Henrietta Street, London WC2E 8PS

2 4 6 8 10 9 7 5 3

A CIP catalogue record for this book is available from the British Library.
ISBN 0 7513 0753 X

Reproduced by Colourscan, Singapore
Printed and bound by Star Standard Industries, Singapore

CONTENTS

WALLS AND FENCES IN THE GARDEN

WHY HAVE WALLS AND FENCES?

W ALLS AND FENCES are so commonplace that they are all too easily relegated to the category of "serviceable necessities" as they perform their invaluable role of enclosing a garden and areas within it. To regard these structures as purely utilitarian, however, greatly underestimates their contribution to the overall look of the garden: with just a little imagination, walls and fences can enhance a garden's design in ways that can be as stylish as they are practical.

PRACTICAL OR DECORATIVE USE?

In a crowded world, the natural desire for privacy is frequently uppermost in the minds of homeowners. This is especially true of the garden, which so often provides a retreat from the hurly-burly of modern life. At a basic level, walls and fences fulfil this need in a practical way as well as providing security, shelter, and a means of dividing a garden site. But practical uses need not exclude decorative appeal: the range of attractive materials and styles available is so diverse that making a suitable choice can seem positively bewildering. A simple listing of your priorities, which takes into account factors such as cost, durability, and style, will help to ensure that you get it right first time.

PAINTED WALL *Reflecting light and maximizing radiated warmth, this white-painted, high brick wall alleviates the potential gloom of a shady, private courtyard to the advantage of both gardener and the plants growing at the wall's base. The wall will require repainting from time to time if its benefits are to be maintained.*

◄ PICKET FENCE *A white picket fence sets off a cottage-style scheme of aquilegias and foxgloves.*

PRACTICAL USES

THE DECISION TO BUILD A NEW WALL OR FENCE in a garden is often made primarily for practical reasons – for example to mark a boundary or to screen the garden from the outside world. Whatever the main purpose, however, the form and strength of the structure, and the construction methods used, must be capable of withstanding the demands made upon it, bearing in mind that some materials and methods are better suited to specific uses than others.

SECURITY AND PRIVACY

A well-built, high brick or stone wall that is impervious to prying eyes includes among its many advantages the highest possible value in terms of good looks, privacy, and security. You need to consider its position carefully, however, (and more so in some neighbourhoods than others) so that in gaining a deterrent to intruders you do not, at the same time, inadvertently provide them with safe cover.

While the initial outlay on materials and labour for a brick- or stone-built wall can be great, long-term maintenance costs are satisfyingly low, and you may even find that it adds to the value of the property.

Where the big outlay on a high wall is out of the question, there are many forms of attractive timber fencing that will do the job just as adequately. Timber fences are not only less expensive in materials, they are also far less demanding in terms of specialist building skills, and offer great savings in labour costs, since the building and installation of most can be undertaken with a minimum of expertise.

PROVIDING WIND PROTECTION

Creating shelter from cold winds can make a garden more comfortable for people and plants alike but, although a high wall may seem ideal for this purpose, it does have one major disadvantage: such a solid barrier often creates vortices in its lee,

ON THE DIAGONAL
Although providing less privacy than a wall or closeboarded panels, this timber fence offers a semi-open method of screening areas of the garden that is particularly useful in windy situations. A dynamic decorative effect is achieved by attaching the boards diagonally across the panels, which are then painted a soft, harmonizing green.

especially in exposed areas. In such cases, consider a semipermeable structure, such as a stout trellis fence. Such a wind filter provides shelter by reducing wind speed – an effect that is enhanced by clothing the fence in climbing plants (*see pp.28–29*).

> Terrace walls transform a difficult site into a new planting opportunity

CHANGING LEVELS
On sloping sites, the use of retaining walls to create terraces provides an interesting way of changing levels while transforming difficult conditions into new planting opportunities. On a flat site, raised beds lend the opportunity of introducing height to a design. Their excellent drainage can prove an ideal solution in gardens with poorly drained soils, and they have the added advantage of bringing plants closer to eye level and to a comfortable working height for gardeners of restricted mobility.

▲ BLUE LATTICEWORK
A latticework effect is achieved in this blue-painted fence of narrow, diagonal trellis panels. The open style provides a form of screening that reduces the impact of windflow.

▼ EASY-REACH RAISED BED
A raised bed of reconstituted stone with brick coping brings this planting scheme to a comfortable working height, and ensures that the plants can be enjoyed at closer quarters.

DECORATIVE USES

A N OLD GARDENING MAXIM directs the designer always to combine use with beauty, and few garden structures offer such great opportunities to put this advice into practice as walls and fences. So great is the wealth of materials available – whether traditional or modern, bought or reclaimed – that walls and fences can be constructed to enhance and decorate gardens in stylish and individual ways that are as beautiful as they are functional.

CREATE A BACKDROP

The sheltering warmth and subtle colour tones of a mellow brick or aged stone wall have long been appreciated as a visually pleasing backdrop to a planting scheme. Not only do they lend valuable height to a design, but they also form the ideal background for displaying climbing plants to perfection. Because they absorb the sun's heat by day and release it by night, walls offer a degree of frost protection in winter, while their additional warmth helps ripen wood during summer, greatly improving flowering potential to fine decorative effect.

A timber fence can play a similar role, whether it is allowed to mellow naturally or is stained or painted with modern timber treatments. The latter are available in a range of colours from the subtle and natural to bright and vibrant finishes.

MYSTERY AND ENTICEMENT

Few of us can resist the invitation, when offered, to explore a garden that is merely glimpsed through a gate or archway set into a wall. With imagination, walls and fences lend infinite possibilities for adding an element of irresistible mystery to a design, screening off one area of the garden

VIBRANT SHAPES AND COLOURS
A harlequin effect is achieved in this blue-stained backdrop of pointed pickets, from which diamond shapes have been cut.

▲ PEEPSHOW
A circular peephole, built into a high brick wall, offers an enticing glimpse into the garden beyond.

◄ SERPENTINE WALL
A gently curved wall creates sheltered bays within the border for surpise displays of choice or favourite plants.

from another so that all is not viewed at once. Try the architects' trick of fenestration – including "peepholes" or *clair voyées* – to frame a view or allow tantalizing glimpses; or simply employ a see-through structure, such as trellis, to give an enticing hint of what lies beyond.

The serpentine or "crinkle-crankle" wall, which was used in old gardens to create warm bays to ripen fruit, lends itself to

Peepholes offer tantalizing glimpses of the view beyond

reinterpretations for smaller gardens. Use the hidden bays as frames for favourite plants, and to add an element of surprise with a succession of cameo plantings.

SPACE DIVIDERS AND SCREENS

Many of the grandest gardens in history use walls and fences as interior dividers of space within the garden. It is a sound principle, even in spaces of more modest scale. Walls or fences can be used to create enclosed garden spaces to suit different activities – for example, to separate the vigorous games-players from the dedicated gardeners of the household, or to separate areas for growing edible crops from more ornamental plantings. They might be used to enclose sheltered areas from the rest of the garden, creating an area for quiet and restful contemplation, or to screen from view unsightly features that lie beyond the garden's boundaries.

In terms of dividing space within a garden, walls and fences play a vital role in creating garden "rooms" for planting designs of different feel and style and are invaluable in remoulding difficult shapes, such as a long, narrow garden, into more pleasing proportions.

Last, but by no means least, walls and fences are indispensable for disguising those mundane, necessary, but aesthetically unappealing items – dustbins, compost heaps, and tool stores – that are inevitable inclusions in most modern gardens.

FENCING TYPES AND MATERIALS

WHETHER IT IS PRIVACY, SECURITY, or simply a boundary marker that you need, there is a type of fencing to fit the bill. At one time, only a restricted palette of brown was on offer, but modern timber treatments have introduced a wealth of colours to tone or contrast with your planting schemes. If you can't find anything you like at the garden centre or do-it-yourself store, you can adapt the techniques to different materials to produce your own, highly individual design statement.

WHY CHOOSE TIMBER FENCING?

In terms of cost and ease of construction, timber fences win outright in comparison with brick or stone. Since they demand little in the way of specialist building skills, you can confidently "do-it-yourself" and make considerable savings on labour costs.

PANEL FENCING

Fencing falls into two broad categories: those made from prefabricated panels, like larch-lap fencing, and those made up of smaller units, such as post-and-rail or picket fences – but there are many variations on each of these themes.

Most prefabricated panels are made up of slats of larch or pine, either interwoven in a basket-weave pattern or horizontally overlapping, as in waney-edged fencing. Tall and visually opaque, they provide instant privacy and some shelter, but lack the necessary structural strength for security purposes. For this, a better choice

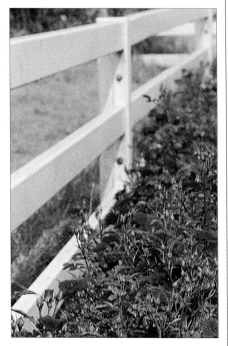

▲ POST-AND-RAIL BOUNDARY
Horizontal rails secured to timber uprights make a neat and simple boundary fence, but offer little in the way of security.

◀ UNOBTRUSIVE CHAINLINK
Plastic-coated chainlink fencing provides a secure barrier that blends into the background when clothed with climbing plants.

▲ SITE DIVIDER
A low panel fence is ideal for dividing the garden into different areas and creates an effective barrier to small animals.

◄ WIND-FILTERING LATTICE
Woven panels provide wind-filtering shelter and a modicum of privacy but lack the structural strength needed for security.

is closeboard fencing (*see pp.36–41*), which is made from overlapping feathered boards or butt-jointed planks. Both can be built from scratch or from prefabricated panels.

LOW AND OPEN FENCING

In gardens that simply need a boundary fence, or in areas with legal restrictions on fence heights, post-and-rail, post-and-chain, or picket-style fencing are relatively inexpensive options. These offer little privacy or security, and the more open the

> Remember, the more open the fence, the less security it will offer

structure, the less suitable it is for keeping the neighbour's dog out of your garden. If the last is high on your wish-list, consider a low panel or closeboard fence. Where appearance is less important, a chainlink fence forms a very effective barrier and can be camouflaged by growing a vigorous climber through it.

▲ SECURITY AND PRIVACY
A closeboard fence provides security and privacy, while the pale green finish forms a subtle background to a planting scheme.

SELECTING A STYLE

Style is partly a matter of personal taste, but the most pleasing results are generally achieved by erecting a fence that suits both setting and purpose. Compare the different moods of an informal rural garden, set amidst rolling countryside, and the neat plot of a suburban villa or a formally minimalist urban courtyard. The first may

> ### For the most pleasing results, select a style to suit the setting

require a stockproof, parkland-style fence that permits unrestricted views of the countryside beyond, but the priority in a suburban plot might be the peep-proof privacy of close-woven panel fencing. In an urban setting, where the strong, geometric lines of nearby buildings dictate a more formal mood, the smooth-planed verticals of a closeboard fence will dovetail perfectly with the surroundings.

▲ RUSTIC CHARM
A fence made of rustic poles provides privacy in a semirural setting while allowing gentle breezes to filter through to the quiet patio area.

▶ RECLAMATION
Old railway sleepers can be used to build a robust, ecologically friendly fence that is particularly suited to large, country spaces. Their well-weathered appearance allows them to look instantly at home.

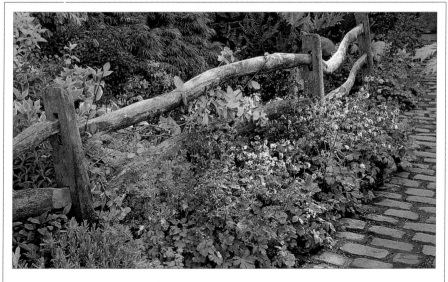

Picket fences, with all their variations of height and pattern, are among the most versatile of fences, suiting both rural and suburban plots. But whereas a rough-hewn picket fence provides the perfect frame for an informal cottage garden, its urban counterpart may be better made of neatly planed timber painted a clean, crisp white. It is worth bearing in mind the powerful mood-enhancing qualities of colour: bright blues and zingy violets may lift the spirits in a modern urban setting, but more pastoral plots almost beg the use of softer sage-greys and holly-greens.

RECLAIMED MATERIALS
Recycling materials makes sound economic and ecological sense, and architectural salvage centres offer a rich source of unique materials. The mellow, weathered appearance of reclaimed timber has the advantage of looking as if it has been in place forever, but you do need to choose materials with care. While a chunky, rough timber fence looks perfectly at home in a large rural garden, and a silver-toned fence made of driftwood forms a perfect frame in a seaside setting, both would look out of place on a modern housing estate.

▲ COTTAGE GARDEN SIMPLICITY
A post-and-rail fence, constructed from mellowed rustic poles, blends easily with a relaxed, cottage-garden-style planting of aquilegias and geraniums.

▼ TEMPORARY MEASURES
Ready-made lengths of chestnut paling form a cheap and instant temporary fence while awaiting full foliage cover from plantings.

VARIATIONS ON A THEME

Observing how gardeners use fencing materials in other parts of the world can be a rich source of inspiration. Think of Japanese gardens, for example, where the soft, neutral colours of bamboo screens form an elegant backdrop to the vertical lines of living bamboos, and tone quite naturally with rocks and gravel. You can

Reinforce the overall garden style with fencing detail

identify and use such stylish elements to lend an oriental feel to your own designs.

In a similar vein, you might vary the shape of picket-fence pales to pick up and echo decorative detail from the house – for example from an existing porch or ornate bargeboard. Fencing detail might reinforce the style of a colonial or Gothic house or, if you use a more local idiom, harmoniously blend a village house and garden with its surroundings. Such attention to detail lends a valuable element of unity to the overall garden design.

▲ BAMBOO SCREENS
The neutral tones of a bamboo screen provide a perfect backdrop to the rich greens of living plants and add an element of oriental style.

▼ ORNATE PICKET FENCING
Many variations of picket fencing are possible. Here, the sculpted zigzag top of the fence is echoed in the ornamental shaping of the pales.

▲ OPEN-PATTERN TRELLIS
Open trellis forms a sturdy
screen without restricting
views of surrounding areas.

◀ CLOSE-PATTERN TRELLIS
This semisolid barrier lends
wind shelter and privacy as
well as adding an element of
mystery to the view beyond.

ADAPTING STYLE TO PURPOSE

You may sometimes find that the style of
fence that you've set your heart on does
not accord with your other priorities. If,
for instance, you love the idea of trellis
work but also need wind shelter and
privacy, instead of an open-pattern trellis,
consider using a more solidly made, close-
textured trellis (*see above*). Alternatively,
attach a panel of trellis to the top of a
more solid structure, such as a closeboard
fence. Other mixed-media techniques
include topping a low stone or brick wall
with trellis or, as shown here (*right*), a
short picket atop a low wall. This is an
economical way of building a strong
barrier that still allows views in and out.

USING TIMBER OUTDOORS

All outdoor timber must be treated with
preservative. Most purchased timber is
already pressure-treated and subsequently
needs only the occasional treatment to
maintain it. The most common form of
pressure treatments impart a green tinge to
the wood, which is easily disguised with a
special, exterior formula "microporous"

wood paint (for opaque colour) or wood
stain (for translucent effects that enhance
the grain). Most also include preservative.
If you prefer a natural wood finish, seek
out special landscape timber that has been
pressure treated with clear preservative.
Protect vulnerable end grain (at the cut
ends of planks or posts) with special coping
rails or weather caps (*see p.41*).

▼ ROUGH TIMBER PICKET
A low slate wall finished with picket fencing
provides a substantial boundary that blends
perfectly into the local landscape.

WALLING TYPES AND MATERIALS

B OUNDARY WALLS HAVE BEEN USED to demarcate and protect gardens since land was first enclosed for cultivation, and reached their zenith in the walled gardens of the Victorian era. While such tall, expensive features have largely been replaced by less costly timber fences, the decorative and practical advantages of smaller walls have been brought well within the scope of the competent homeowner by the wealth of modern materials available and their relative ease of construction.

CHOOSING THE RIGHT MATERIALS

Walling materials fall into three broad groups: stone, brick, and concrete. Each has many variations. Some require high levels of skill to produce a result that will please you throughout a wall's long life so, if you intend to do it yourself, be realistic in your aspirations and match the ease of construction with your own level of skill. Consider, too, how well the colour and texture of your possible choices will blend with your home and its setting and whether they will give the look you have in mind.

STONE WALLING

Natural stone walls are made from dressed, rough-dressed, or undressed stone: all are obtainable from a stone merchant or local quarry. Whether laid dry or jointed with mortar, stone walls are costly but hard to beat if you want an informal wall that blends seamlessly into its environment.

Dry-stone walls are usually made from rough- or undressed stone. Both demand time and skill in construction as the wall's ultimate strength depends on each stone fitting snugly with its neighbour, like the pieces of a jigsaw. In areas with a tradition of dry-stone walls, you can often find weekend courses to learn the basics.

DRY-STONE WALL
This dry-stone wall illustrates how stones of different shapes and sizes are dovetailed to form a wall whose strength does not rely on mortar. Its intricate construction is both highly skilled and time consuming.

Dressed stone is more costly, but it is the easiest of natural materials to use as it is shaped for uniformity. If the high cost is out of the question, however, you might try reconstituted stone. The best is almost indistinguishable from the real thing, and construction is as simple as laying bricks, producing a perfect effect where a formal, uniform finish is wanted.

KIT-FORM STONE WALLING
If ease of construction is paramount, try a kit form of dry-stone walling, which gives realistic results with minimal skill.

> It is easy to locate a type of brick to suit your particular setting

▲ RECONSTITUTED STONE
Preformed blocks of reconstituted stone are simple to put together and much cheaper than quarried stone. Here, they make both a raised bed and a high wall that absorbs traffic noise.

BRICK WALLS
The uniform shape and size of bricks makes construction relatively easy and produces a result that is well suited to formal designs.

The colour, finish, and durability of a brick wall is dictated by the type of clay and processes used in the manufacture of the bricks. Clay colour shows considerable local variation, and it is easy to locate a type to suit your local setting. Bricks are rated according to strength and weather resistance, so it is important to check that your choice is suitable for the job in hand.

Brick walls must be finished with coping to prevent water penetration from above and the damage that would be caused by subsequent freezing and thawing.

◄ WEATHERED BRICK
A brick wall in a damp, shady site attracts moss and lichen and will weather attractively.

▼ PROTECTIVE COPING
Coping prevents rain seeping into the wall; a stone sphere adds the finishing touch.

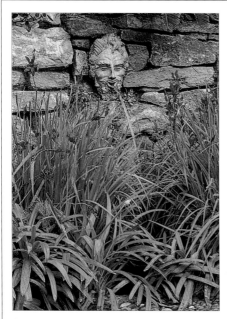

▲ FOUNTAIN NICHE
Adding the vitality of moving water to the design – and delighting the irises growing below – a sandstone Neptune water spout is built into a niche in this dry-stone wall.

▼ BOLDLY MODERN
A blue-painted stuccoed wall, topped by a picket fence of the same colour, makes a strikingly modern backdrop to the plants in this courtyard garden.

HARMONIZING DETAILS

The construction of brick and stone walls provides an opportunity to incorporate design details that will dovetail them firmly into their setting, whether this be in choice of materials and style, or as an echo of vernacular architecture.

Stone does this in an obvious way. For example, if the native bedrock comprises flint or sandstone, then walls made of the same materials will blend naturally into the landscape. You might also want to include one of the many regional variations in coping or capping styles.

The bonding patterns of brickwork (*see p.52*), although often used simply for their structural strength or decorative quality, may also be chosen because they reflect either the building tradition in an area or an historical architectural period.

VERSATILE CONCRETE

Concrete has an unfortunate utilitarian image – due, perhaps, to its immense strength and widespread use in industry. Nevertheless, with just a little imagination, concrete can be one of the most practical and versatile of walling materials.

Concrete blocks are among the cheapest of hard materials, and their uniformity and relatively large unit size make for quick and

STUCCO AND APPLIED SHELL ART
A stylized pattern, created with mussel and cockle shells, has been applied to the terracotta-coloured stucco on this stone wall. A variegated ivy creeps up to join the blue flower motif.

simple construction. Disguising their appearance can be achieved in a variety of ways: the most common is to use a veneer of beautifully finished facing bricks, which reduces the cost in comparison with an all-brick wall without compromising structural strength. Dressed stone can be used in a similar way. When finished with a brick or stone capping, a concrete wall is almost indistinguishable from the real thing.

> Alcoves provide a frame for focal features such as statuary and fountains

Perhaps the most versatile disguise is a stucco veneer. This mixture of masonry cement and fine sand can be patterned by scoring, brushing, or imprinting, or adorned with applied decoration. Stucco can also be painted with exterior masonry paint. White or honey tones lend a Mediterranean feel to a design, while brighter colours can transform a dingy urban yard into a vibrant, thoroughly modern design feature. Do check, however, that the colours you choose accord with local legal restrictions.

FOCAL FEATURES
Walls constructed of brick, stone, or concrete are infinitely more versatile than timber constructions when it comes to incorporating alcoves designed to frame focal features such as a piece of statuary, a water fountain, or a choice specimen plant.

Sheltered niches are the ideal location for plants that need a little extra warmth; alcoves also make a perfect frame for decorative fruit-tree forms, such as fans or espaliers, and provide valuable protection during the vulnerable flowering and fruit-setting period.

SECURE FIXINGS
Solid walls provide a secure and durable fixing surface for a fountain spout. The sight and sound of moving water adds a thrilling dimension to a garden design, approaching perfection when the materials blend harmoniously or contrast subtly with each other (*see facing page, above*).

▶ SEASIDE THEME
A fan-shaped insert of scallop shells provides variation in colour and texture to the dark-coloured stones in a seaside garden's dry-stone wall.

▼ GLEAMING GLASS
Green glass bottle ends embedded in a brick wall enliven its uniformity by adding both colour and an attractive, translucent gleam to the surface.

you might incorporate a fine-textured mosaic of small, smooth pebbles gleaned from holiday beaches over the years.

Such decorative touches can also provide a simple but effective means of emphasizing a garden style: a scallop-shell mosaic (*see above*) or a collection of seaside fossils, for example, could reinforce the theme of a coastal garden.

FOUND MATERIALS

Designs that include found or reclaimed materials are easy on both the eye and the pocket and often carry with them the added satisfaction of creating a unique structure. Pieces of water-worn glass from

APPLIED DECORATION

Perhaps more than any other technique, the application of a decorative finish to a wall's surface provides a means of stamping your own, individual identity on the design. You might, for example, use the opportunity to include elements that represent events in your family history, thus making a highly personal and permanent memento.

Champagne bottle bottoms incorporated into a wall, as shown above, could mark a series of family celebrations while, at the same time, introducing a translucent gleam to an otherwise functional structure. Or

Create a unique design by incorporating found materials into a wall

beach or river bed, shards of pottery found during garden digging, or chunks of mason-worked stone from the architectural salvage merchant can all be used for added decorative interest. Or you could use rough chunks of found rock crystals and glass nuggets, in the time-honoured fashion, to create a grotto effect.

Since the most appealing results are usually achieved by restricting intense detail to relatively small areas, you can even justify the purchase of costly materials such as brilliantly coloured ceramic or tiny mirror tiles; these would be prohibitively expensive if used on a large scale, but you can often find such precious oddments in end-of-line sales.

This technique is perfect for imparting a Moorish style to your designs – for example by creating miniature mosaic panels set against a lapis-blue background, as shown below. If you're really ambitious, you can apply pictorial mosaics in the style of a Romanesque fresco. Almost any durable material can be used, but rough-textured items give the strongest bond.

Successful Application

Planning ahead is vital to the success of such detailed work, so mark out your design on graph paper before you start and sort your materials by texture and colour. Embed applied materials to at least two-thirds of their depth in a stucco or cement surface: a builder's float is the ideal tool for this and gives a fairly level finish. Work on a small area at a time, so that the cement does not dry before you finish. When the concrete is firm, reveal the final beauty by removing excess concrete with a stiff-bristled brush and a spray of clean water.

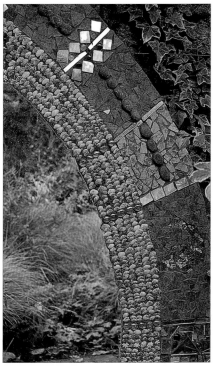

▲ MIRROR-TILE MOSAIC
A trompe l'oeil effect of depth and distance is achieved here by the application of a mirror-tile mosaic that reflects the border planting.

▼ MOORISH INFLUENCE
Mosaic detail on the lapis-blue ground of a courtyard wall evokes an atmosphere of Mediterranean sun and warmth.

Practical Considerations

WHETHER THE INTENDED PURPOSE of your wall or fence is simply a boundary marker or to provide a more substantial or decorative structure, you will have thought through the suitability, desirability, and cost of the proposed materials and design. But before ordering materials and beginning the physical labour of building your wall or fence, there are a number of factors to be considered to ensure that your project is legal, safe, and easily manageable.

Legal Aspects

In most areas, the law concerning the construction of garden walls and fences is essentially very simple. Structures adjacent to a public highway must be no higher than 1m (3ft) above ground level; elsewhere, they can be up to 2m (6ft) in height. Anything more substantial requires planning consent. You must, of course, also ensure that the structure lies within the boundaries of your property.

If you're lucky enough to live in a conservation area, there may be local restrictions on the colour and style of walls and fences; and, if your home is a listed building, the methods and materials used must not have adverse impact upon it. In either case – and if you have any doubts at all – consult your local building control or planning officer before you begin: they are a primary source of expert advice. Bear in mind that they are also empowered to order the removal of structures that contravene regulations.

Your local planning officer is a prime source of expert advice

Safety Considerations

Building materials are heavy so, when lifting, take due care to hold the weight close to your body, keep your back straight, and let your thigh muscles take the strain (see p.65). Wear sturdy boots and use protective gloves, especially when working with cement and mortar and

FLATTERING FOLIAGE
A high brick wall provides long-lasting, low-maintenance, effective security, but its construction is usually a job for a professional builder. To soften the brash look of new red brick, grow shrubs such as Cytisus battandieri *up and over the wall.*

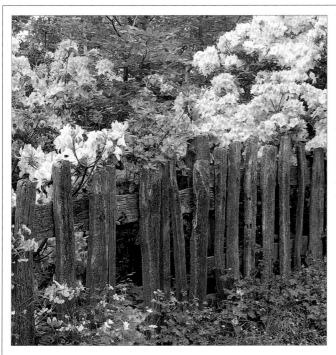

INNATE CHARM
With dense planting on the other side creating an effective deterrent barrier, it hardly matters that this tumbledown, rustic picket fence provides little in the way of security: its immense visual charm more than makes up for the lack of functional strength.

handling rough stones and brick. If you are cutting brick or stone, protect your eyes with goggles and, when using electrical tools outdoors, ensure that they are fitted with a residual current device (RCD).

STRUCTURAL SAFETY

Walls need firm foundations to support and distribute their weight; their depth depends on the size of wall (*see p.66*). A single-course wall (half a brick thick) should be no higher than 70cm (28in); anything taller requires a double course. As a rule, walls higher than 1m (3ft) need the additional strength of built-in piers. The greater level of technical skills demanded by higher walls is beyond the scope of most amateurs so, in this case, call in the professionals.

CHOOSING A PROFESSIONAL

Personal recommendation is the safest and simplest route to finding a reliable builder. Failing that, the local garden centre or builder's merchant may have contacts.

When you've made a short list, ask to see samples of completed work, obtain and compare competitive quotations and check whether insurance-backed guarantees are offered. The latter ensures that any failure is the builder's responsibility, not yours. Finally, draw up a written contract to agree the nature of the work, proposed timescale, and terms of payment.

BE PREPARED

- Building materials are both heavy and high volume: wherever possible arrange delivery directly to the site and recruit a team of willing helpers to help shift materials.
- Bricks and cement must be kept dry, so have ready a wooden pallet to keep them off the ground and cover them with watertight polythene or a tarpaulin until required.
- If you live in a terrace and have to carry materials through the house, take steps to protect interior walls and surfaces.
- Building work is hard, physical labour so, if you're unused to exercise, warm up first to reduce the risk of strains or sprains.

PLANTING BY WALLS AND FENCES

So DIVERSE ARE THE NEW PLANTING SITES created by the introduction of a wall or fence into the garden that a keen gardener may build one just to take advantage of these opportunities. To maximize the use of such structures, however, and to make the most successful choice of plants that will flourish in the conditions created, a little forethought and some understanding of the ways in which walls and fences influence the surrounding microclimates is required.

SUN, SHADE, AND RAIN SHADOW

If you look at the base of a wall just after a shower, you will see clearly the effects of rain shadow. In an area up to 45cm (18in) from the base, the soil will be drier than that which lies just beyond. This is why wall-trained shrubs and climbers, which need moisture for good growth, must be planted at least 45cm (18in) away from the wall's base. But this doesn't mean that rain-shadow areas are unsuitable for planting: they are, in fact, the perfect site for bulbs (such as nerines or *Amaryllis belladonna*) that require hot, dry summers for good flowering.

The reflected warmth from the sunniest walls often creates local hot spots. Some plants, such as meconopsis or primulas, find such sites unendurable, but there are many plants that thrive in the heat. Grey-leaved plants – like santolinas, salvias, and some artemisias – or Mediterranean natives, such as *Cytisus battandieri* or rock roses (*Helianthemum*) are perfectly adapted to these conditions and often justify their inclusion by flowering more freely here.

Every sunny wall has its shady side, but shade is not a problem: it's an opportunity to increase the range of plants you grow. In damp shade, shade-lovers produce lush growth, retain their colour, and remain in peak condition for longer periods. Some will even tolerate dry shade: choose these for the rain-shadowed base of a shady wall.

▲ HOT, DRY AREA
Soil in the lee of a sunny wall is hot and sheltered from rain, requiring extra care in the choice and maintenance of plants.

▲ SPEEDY COVERAGE
*Golden hop (*Humulus lupulus* 'Aureus') will rapidly smother an unsightly wall or fence with its bright yellow foliage.*

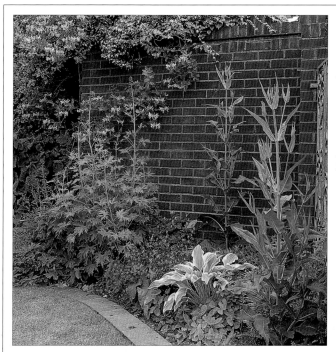

SHADY AREA
A high brick wall blocks out light in this corner but provides the perfect conditions for shade-tolerant plants. Many of these give a lush display that continues to look good when plants in sunny positions are past their best.

Frost Pockets

Cold air behaves just like water – it flows downhill and accumulates in the lowest-lying hollows to create what is known as frost pockets. If air flow is unimpeded, the potential cold damage caused to plants is minimized, but a wall or fence at the bottom of slope acts as a barrier to the

Shade provides an opportunity to grow a wider range of plants

flow and risks creating a frost pocket. This likelihood is reduced if permeable fences such as picket are used, but it is sometimes unavoidable. Do not despair: cold areas are not "no-go" areas for planting. You need simply choose plants from the many that are reliably cold hardy; these are often plants that don't emerge until late in spring when danger of severe frosts has passed.

SUITABLE PLANTS

HOT SPOTS

Crinum x powellii Fragrant, funnel-shaped, showy pink flowers in late summer.
Phlomis italica Grey-leaved subshrub with pink flower spikes in summer.
Rosmarinus officinalis (**Rosemary**) Aromatic evergreen shrub with blue flowers in spring.
Salvia officinalis (**Sage**) Aromatic grey foliage and spikes of blue flowers in summer.
Stachys byzantina (**Lamb's tongue**) Silver-grey leaves and woolly flower spikes in summer.

DRY SHADE

Alchemilla mollis Lime-green foliage and sprays of tiny yellow flowers in summer.
Iris foetidissima Seed pods split in autumn to reveal shiny orange-red seeds.
Liriope muscari Evergreen leaves and spikes of tiny purple flowers in autumn.
Symphytum ibericum Robust ground cover with pale yellow flowers in late spring.
Tellima grandiflora Ground cover with long-lived spikes of pale green flowers in summer.
Tolmeia menziesii 'Taff's Gold' Ground cover with gold-and-cream-mottled leaves.

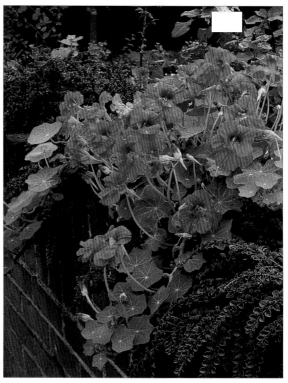

▲ ROCK PLANTS
Crevices in a stone wall provide ideal conditions for a variety of rock plants, including echeveria, as drainage is good and the plants enjoy a cool root run.

▶ CLIMBERS AND TRAILERS
Walls provide excellent opportunities for both trailing and climbing plants. Here, orange nasturtiums tumble over the tiered branches of Cotoneaster horizontalis.

PLANTS FOR RAPID COVER

Although it's often best to train wall plants over several seasons, more rapid cover will be needed if you inherit an unsightly wall or wish to clothe a chainlink fence to form a peep-proof barrier. If you need temporary cover while permanent plantings establish, try quick-growing annuals, such as sweet peas (*Lathyrus odorata*) or *Eccremocarpus scaber*, or perennials, such as the golden-leaved hop (*Humulus lupulus* 'Aureus').

For permanent cover, choose woody stemmed climbers, but remember that only evergreens will be effective all year round.

SUPPORTING CLIMBERS

Different types of climber require different types of support. Self-clinging climbers, like ivy (*Hedera*) or parthenocissus, have adhesive pads that stick to any surface that offers purchase, such as masonry, wood, or

tree bark. They need initial guidance to a wall or fence, then become self-supporting. Twiners, tendril-climbers, and scramblers, like wisteria, clematis, or winter jasmine (*Jasminum nudiflorum*), need a permanent support such as wires and vine eyes or trellis. Scramblers will need tying in throughout their life, but twiners and tendril-climbers attach themselves firmly to their support once they are established.

All supports must be strong enough to bear the weight of the mature plant, and should be fixed 10–15cm (4–6in) away from the wall to ensure good air circulation and minimize the risk of fungal diseases.

CHOOSING WALL PLANTS

Walls provide the ideal habitat not just for the obvious climbers and wall shrubs but for a whole range of plant groups. A hollow wall can be planted with trailers, such as *Lithodora diffusa, Aurinia saxatilis,* or even ground-cover roses to cascade down the face, while the crevices in a dry-stone wall are ideal for rock plants, especially cushion formers that revel in perfect drainage. Shade lovers, like lewisias,

---

A sunny dry stone wall provides perfect niches for many rock plants

---

thrive on the shady side of a wall.

As well as plants that enjoy the added warmth of a wall, the most successful wall shrubs are those with long, flexible stems, such as honeysuckle, those that tolerate clipping to shape, like pyracantha, and shrubs with a two-dimensional habit, such as *Cotoneaster horizontalis,* with its fans of horizontally tiered branches.

PLANTS FOR RAPID COVER

ANNUALS AND PERENNIALS

Cobaea scandens Bell-shaped green-white flowers age to purple in summer to autumn.
Eccremocarpus scaber Tubular yellow-orange flowers from early summer to autumn.
***Humulus lupulus* 'Aureus' (Golden hop)** Golden foliage and attractive fruits.
***Lathyrus odorata* (Sweet pea)** Scented flowers ranging from pure white, through pink and mauve, to deep purple in summer.
***Tropaeolum peregrinum* (Nasturtium)** Canary-yellow flowers all summer.

WOODY-STEMMED CLIMBERS

Clematis montana Pink or white flowers from spring to early summer.
Fallopia baldschuanica Rampant climber with sprays of white flowers in late summer.
***Lonicera periclymenum* (Honeysuckle)** Fragrant yellow or white and pink flowers mid- to late summer.
Vitis coignetiae Large sculptural leaves with orange, red, and yellow autumn tints.

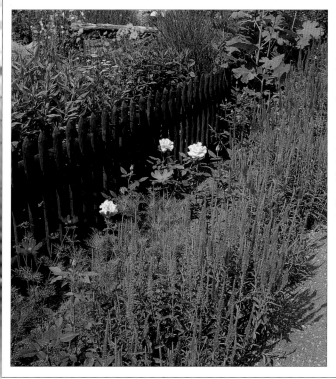

SHARED FENCING
A colourful display of herbaceous perennials provides a cheerful aspect for neighbours on either side of a picket fence. If you wish to grow a climber on a shared boundary such as this, it would be courteous to consult your neighbours first. You might even persuade them to share pruning duties.

FENCES IN THE GARDEN

TIMBER FENCES

Timber-built fences are relatively quick and simple to erect, using readily available materials and demanding little in the way of specialist building skills. They can provide almost instant privacy and wind shelter, and are among the most commonly used structures as boundary markers. Equally importantly, fences offer great potential as decorative garden features, whether painted or stained, or harmoniously clothed with wall shrubs and climbers.

MAKING A PANEL FENCE

Panel fences are among the easiest of installations: pre-fabricated panels are simply attached to a series of timber or concrete uprights. Timber posts have the aesthetic edge, but they are prone to rot and require regular maintenance throughout their life. Concrete posts are grooved, so slotting panels in place is child's play, both during the initial construction and later, should any damaged panels need replacing.

Concrete post

Fence panel

Gravel board of timber or preformed concrete

Hardcore base topped with concrete

PRACTICAL HINTS
• For longevity and low maintenance, choose concrete posts and gravel boards.
• Apply a coat of liquid manure to encourage lichen growth on stark new concrete.

CONSTRUCTION OF A PANEL FENCE
A pre-fabricated panel is slotted into concrete posts. The gravel board protects the panel from rotting by preventing contact with the soil.

◀ ADDING HEIGHT *A hedge of* Cotoneaster lacteus *increases both privacy and shelter.*

YOU NEED:

TOOLS
- String and pegs
- Measuring tape
- Spade
- Spirit level
- Claw hammer
- Paintbrush

MATERIALS
- Hardcore and concrete for setting posts in place
- 10cm (4in) square concrete posts
- 2 x 2m (6ft) fence panels
- Preformed concrete gravel boards
- Timber capping rail
- Timber preservative
- Galvanized nails

ERECTING THE FENCE POSTS

1 Mark out the fence line with string and pegs. Dig a 75cm- (30in-) deep hole and pack a 15cm- (6in-) layer of hardcore in the base. Set a concrete post in place. Check its height against the panel. Adjust height, adding more hardcore as necessary.

2 Place a spirit level against the concrete post to check that it is vertical. Pack more hardcore around the post to hold it in place, then check again that it is vertical.

3 Pour concrete into the hole around the post. Tamp down with a timber offcut to dispel air bubbles. Keep adding and tamping concrete until it is just below ground level.

POSITIONING THE PANEL AND FINISHING OFF

4 **Lay the panel** on the ground with the base against the string line. Mark the position of the next hole, making allowances for the depth of the grooves in the posts.

5 **Dig a hole** for the second post and fill with a 15cm- (6in-) layer of hardcore. Slot the gravel board into the groove in the post; adjust the soil level so the board is horizontal.

6 **Fit the panel** into the groove in the first post, above the gravel board. Place the second post in the hole and slot the ends of the gravel board and panel into the groove, adjusting the hardcore level as necessary. Pack the post into position with hardcore and fill the hole with concrete as with the first post. Repeat with more panels and posts to the desired length of the fence.

7 **Cut a length** of capping rail to fit the top of each panel and treat the cut ends with timber preservative. Fix the rail to the top of the panel with galvanized nails. The rail protects the end-grain of the panel boards by shedding rainwater away from the fence top.

DEALING WITH SLOPES

Fences on sloping ground can either be built as a series of stepped horizontal runs, or made to slope in line with the ground. As panel fences lose structural strength if cut, they must be stepped. Uprights must be longer than those required on level ground, the extra height depending on the gradient and the width of the panels. The wedge-shaped gap beneath the panel is filled with a gravel board that is shaped to fit (*see below, left*).

Sloping fences are made of boards nailed to rails that run parallel to the slope. The boards sit vertically on the gravel board, with bases angled to match the slope. Use a template to help cut the correct angle.

STEPPED PANEL FENCE
Shaped gravel boards provide a horizontal base for a stepped panel fence. A more weatherproof, although costly, alternative is to build a stepped series of low brick walls between the posts to create a level base.

SLOPING CLOSEBOARD FENCE
With support posts installed vertically in concrete foundations, and cross-rails and gravel board running parallel to the ground, each board is nailed vertically in place, its base angled to match the slope.

LEVELLING A SLOPE

With steeper slopes than those shown above, it is advisable to create a level base between the posts for each panel or fence run. For each section, drive in a stake at the top and bottom of the slope. Stretch a string line between the two and find the horizontal with a builder's line level. Excavate the soil to create a level base that is parallel to the line. Repeat the procedure for each section, to achieve a stepped series of level bases for the fence.

CROSSWAYS SLOPE

If a slope traverses your garden so that your neighbour's land is higher than your own, a timber fence will need to be set on a brick retaining wall to prevent the fence rotting through contact with soil. Legally, such a wall must lie entirely within your property, but you may need access to your neighbour's land to construct it. Avoid any disputes by consulting courteously before work begins.

ALTERNATIVE METHODS OF SUPPORT

There are methods of installing timber posts that reduce rotting by keeping them clear of wet earth. Metal post supports are excellent in stone-free soils; in stony soils, they may bend on impact and are best set in concrete. Use 60cm (24in) supports for fences up to 1.2m (4ft) high; 75cm (30in) for fences up to 2m (6ft) high. In stony soil, you could also use concrete spurs.

USING METAL POST SUPPORTS

1 **Set the fixing** accessory on a timber offcut in the post support socket. Drive the post into the ground with a sledgehammer.

2 **Keep checking** with a spirit level that the post support is vertical. Be sure to check the level on all 4 sides of the support.

3 **Insert the fence** post into the socket at the top of the post support. Secure in place by nailing through the slatted holes with galvanized nails.

SET IN CONCRETE

In stony ground, avoid bending or twisting damage to metal post supports by setting them in a concrete foundation so that the bottom of the support socket sits flush with the ground.

Alternatively, use a concrete spur set in a concrete foundation: this will keep both timber posts and fence panels well clear of damp ground. Spurs are made with pre-drilled holes for bolting the uprights securely to them. Before erecting, match up, mark, and drill corresponding holes in the timber posts.

METAL POST SUPPORT

CONCRETE SPUR

MAKING A CLOSEBOARD FENCE

Closeboard fencing not only offers neat, clean lines that suit both urban and rural settings; it is also one of the strongest forms of fencing and provides almost instant privacy and security.

Pre-fabricated closeboard panels are available but cannot be satisfactorily cut to size, so self-build is the best and simplest option for awkward spaces.

The fence can be finished with wood stain, in natural or vibrant colours, or painted with opaque, exterior-grade microporous wood paints.

PRACTICAL HINTS

• Be sure to provide adequate foundations for uprights: as a general rule, you'll need a 60cm- (24in-) deep hole for fences 1.2–1.5m- (4–5ft-) high, or a 75cm- (30in-) deep hole for a 2m- (6ft-) high fence.
• Always choose pressure-treated timber for outdoor use. Disguise the characteristic green tint with paint or stain, or seek out specialist landscaping timber that has been pressure-treated with a clear preservative. Treat newly cut surfaces with wood preservative.
• Use a spacer gauge, cut to the width of one board minus the overlap, to ensure that each board uniformly overlaps its neighbour.

YOU NEED:

TOOLS
• Measuring tape
• Saw
• Chisel
• Claw hammer
• Paintbrush
• Spade
• Spirit level
• Screwdriver
• Drill

MATERIALS
• 10cm (4in) square timber posts
• 15 x 2.5cm (6 x 1in) timber for gravel board
• 8 x 2.5cm (3 x 1in) timber for cross-rails
• Timber preservative
• Hardcore
• Instant concrete mix
• 15 x 2.5cm (6 x 1in) timber for battens
• Screws
• Galvanized nails
• Feather-edged boards
• Timber capping rail
• Timber post caps

PARTS OF A CLOSEBOARD FENCE

Post cap

Capping rail protects boards from rain damage

Screws

Cross-rail to which boards are nailed

Housing joint

Feather-edged board

Gravel board prevents boards rotting

Batten

Concrete

Timber post

Hardcore base

◀ CLOSEBOARD FENCE *A dark stain provides a fine foil for a flowering almond (*Prunus triloba*).*

PREPARING THE POSTS

1 **Cut the posts** to length: here, 2m (6ft) for a final height of 1.5m (5ft) on 60cm- (24in-) deep foundations. Mark the position for the bottom edge of the gravel board 45cm (18in) from the post base. Rails should sit about 75cm (30in) from the post base and 30cm (12in) below the fence top.

2 **Mark out** on the post the sections to be removed to house the cross-rails. With the post held firmly in a vice, make several saw cuts down to a depth of 2.5cm (1in).

3 **Using a chisel** and hammer, and working away from your body, remove the marked-up timber section. Paint the cut section with timber preservative. Repeat with each post.

SETTING THE POSTS IN INSTANT CONCRETE

1 **Dig a 60cm- (24in-) hole** and pack with 15cm (6in) of hardcore. Position the post with cut sections at the back, checking that it is vertical. Fill the hole with dry concrete mix.

2 **Pour water** over the dry concrete mix according to manufacturer's instructions. Before the concrete has set, check that the post is still vertical, repositioning if necessary.

3 Set the second post in the same way, checking that it is vertical and that its position is accurate for the proposed line of the fence.

4 With both posts in place, put the first cross-rail in position; check that it is horizontal. Make any adjustments that may be necessary.

FIXING THE GRAVEL BOARD AND CROSS-RAILS

1 Using galvanized nails, attach a timber batten to the inner surface of the lower part of each post, placing them so that the gravel board will be flush with the posts.

2 With a spirit level, check that the gravel board is horizontal, making any necessary adjustments. Nail the gravel board to the battens, using 2 nails to each batten.

3 Screw the cross-rails into the prepared housing joints in the support posts, positioning them halfway into the cut sections. Use a hand- or electric drill to make guide holes, then screw cross-rails firmly into place.

ATTACHING THE BOARDS

1 **Mark out** and cut the boards to the required fence height, from the top of the gravel board to 8cm (3in) below the post top.

2 **Position the first** board on top of the gravel board and butt it up against the support post. Fit by tapping the board gently into place.

3 **Attach the board** to the top cross-rail with 2 galvanized nails. Check the level, then fix to lower rail.

4 **Lay a spacer gauge** over the first board; position a second board to overlap the first by 10–12mm (½–⅝in).

5 **Nail the board** to the top rail with 1 galvanized nail. Check that it is vertical, then nail to the bottom rail.

6 **Continue attaching** the remaining boards, using the spacer board to ensure that each board overlaps its neighbour by the same amount. Fix with 1 nail at both top and bottom. Use a string line between the posts as a guide to the position of the nails, and check constantly that the boards are vertical.

FINISHING OFF AND WEATHERPROOFING

1 **Measure and cut** the last board to fit the remaining space, with the broadest edge butted up against the post. Nail into position.

2 **Measure and cut** the capping rail to fit between the posts. Carefully nail into place, through the rail, and into the ends of the boards. Nail a timber post cap to each support post.

VARIATIONS ON THE CLOSEBOARD THEME

Instead of using overlapping, feather-edged boards, a closeboard fence can be made of butt-jointed boards of equal thickness. This produces a fence that is every bit as sturdy, but more versatile in terms of varying the height and width of the boards and adding decorative detail. For example, the boards can be cut to different heights to give a castellated effect, or shaped along the top into serpentine curves. Drilled or cut perforations of diamonds, circles, or even quatrefoils add an individual flourish.

BUTT-BOARD FENCE
A simple butt-board fence takes on elegant detail by introducing a variation in height and a simple, Gothic-style motif of drilled trefoil perforations. The horizontally cut board tops are protected by short lengths of capping rail, and the whole fence treated with timber preservative.

MAKING A PICKET FENCE

In terms of privacy and security, a picket fence is more decorative than functional but, nevertheless, it makes an ideal boundary marker and will certainly keep the neighbour's dog out of your garden.

A simple, white-painted picket is the traditional companion for a clapboard or colonial-style house, while its unpainted counterpart – made from rougher timbers – is a perfect frame for the cottage-style garden. Combine the simplicity of construction with the wealth of modern paint and stain finishes available, however, and the

PRACTICAL HINTS

• If you intend to paint your picket fence, choose planed timber, which has a smoother surface than rough, unplaned boards.
• Use unplaned boards for a more rustic effect; they are cheaper, too.
• Introduce decorative detail by varying pale heights, or by shaping the tops of support posts and individual pales.

picket fence is versatile enough to suit even the most contemporary setting. Ring the changes by alternating long and short pales or, instead of round- or pointed-topped pales, use a jigsaw to create more decorative outlines.

YOU NEED:

TOOLS
• Measuring tape
• Saw
• Sandpaper
• Straightedge
• Set square
• Claw hammer
• Drill
• Screwdriver
• Post driving tool
• Spirit level
• Paintbrush

MATERIALS
• 7.5 x 2.5cm (3 x 1in) planed timber for cross-rails and pales
• Galvanized nails
• Screws
• 7.5cm (3in) fence posts
• 7.5cm (3in) spiked metal post supports
• Coloured wood stain or exterior wood paint

PARTS OF A PICKET FENCE

Galvanized nails are rust-proof

Screws secure cross-rails to posts

Cross-rail

Pales sit clear of ground to avoid rotting

Timber support post

Metal post supports simplify installation of timber support posts

◀ ZIGZAG PICKET *Echoing the pointed tops of pales and posts, the fence is cut into a zigzag shape.*

CUTTING THE PALES

1 **Having decided** on the ultimate fence height, cut the planed timber into pales of the required length.

2 **Make a template** from stiff card for the chosen shape for the top of the pales and mark out each length.

3 **With a saw,** carefully cut the top of the pales to the required shape. Smooth the cut edges with sandpaper.

FIXING PALES TO CROSS-RAILS

1 **Set out the** pales on the ground, using a straight length of timber to align them at the base. Lay the cross-rails at the desired heights and position the first pale at a distance from the ends of the cross-rails to allow for the width of 1 pale plus half the width of the timber support post.

2 **Check the angles** with a set square. Fix the pale to the cross-rails, driving 2 nails diagonally into each rail.

3 **Position the next pale,** using the spacer to determine the correct distance from the first. Attach to the cross-rails as before, with 2 nails top and bottom. Continue to the end, checking that each pale is vertical.

4 **Drill 2 guide holes** at each end of both rails. Screw the rails to the support posts. Shape the tops of the support posts as desired, or use shaped post caps.

FIXING POSTS AND FENCE PANEL

1 Cut the timber posts to length, allowing for the depth of the post-support socket in which the post will sit and the fence's ultimate height above ground level. Lay the panel on the ground in its final position. Place the posts alongside to work out the position for the spiked metal post supports.

2 Using a post driving tool, drive the metal supports into the ground. Insert the posts and check the level on a straightedge laid across them.

3 Screw the cross-rails to the timber posts, using 2 screws at each end of both top and bottom rails.

4 Protect the fence by painting or staining in your chosen colour and finish. The one used here is a coloured wood stain that preserves the timber and adds a vibrant colour, while allowing the grain of the wood to show through.

WALLS IN THE GARDEN

A BRICK WALL MAKES THE PERFECT BOUNDARY to a garden, high walls offering the best possible value in security, privacy, and ornament. If a wall is to be strong and safe, it is vital to make an accurate assessment of your skills before you begin: a simple, low brick wall is a realistic achievement for the competent amateur, but higher, more complex walls are best left to the professionals.

MAKING A FOOTING

The higher a wall, the more substantial its foundations must be. For walls up to 1m (3ft) in height, footings should be two to three times the width of the wall with a depth at least equal to the width of the wall (see table on p.66).

On clay soils or in areas with severe winters, where footings must be below the frost line, it's best to seek expert advice before building. The footing surface must be level, the sides of the trench vertical, and its corners true.

YOU NEED:

TOOLS
- String and pegs
- Measuring tape
- Set square
- Spade
- Straightedge
- Spirit level

MATERIALS
- Hardcore to fill trench to a depth of 15cm (6in)
- Concrete: 1 part cement to 1½ parts sharp sand to 3½ parts aggregate; or 5 parts combined aggregate to 1 part cement, omitting the sand (as on p.48)

STRIP FOUNDATIONS FOR WALLS

1 **Set out** the position of the required foundations with string and pegs. Using a builder's set square, check that all corners are square and true (see p.66).

2 **Dig a trench** of the necessary depth (see above). Drive in pegs to the level for the concrete, checking their alignment with a straightedge and spirit level.

3 **Soak the trench** with water and let it drain. Pack in a 15cm- (6in-) layer of hardcore. Pour in the concrete, slicing with a spade to dispel air bubbles.

4 **Tamp down** the concrete with a length of timber and level it to the top of the pegs. Leave to cure for at least 2 days before starting to build.

◄ A LOW BRICK WALL *A perfect site divider here lends elevation to a display of summer bedding.*

BUILDING A LOW BRICK WALL

For strength and stability, a simple, full-brick wall should be no higher than 1m (3ft). Construction at this height is a realistic do-it-yourself job. Higher walls demand a considerable level of skill and experience. To ensure a uniform finish, use a storey rod as a gauge, marked off at 75mm (3in) intervals (for standard bricks with 10mm- (½in-) mortar joints). For the best results, practise throwing mortar and buttering bricks before you begin.

YOU NEED:

TOOLS
- Builder's lines
- Spirit level
- Builder's trowel
- Storey rod
- Pointing tool
- Bolster chisel
- Club hammer

MATERIALS
- Standard bricks: allow 60 bricks per square metre (50 per square yard)
- Mortar: 1 part cement to 3 parts soft sand; or 50kg (1cwt) pre-mixed mortar per square metre (square yard)

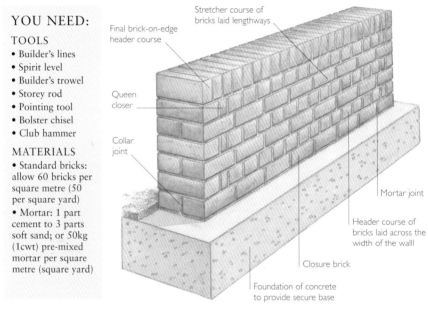

Stretcher course of bricks laid lengthways

Final brick-on-edge header course

Queen closer

Collar joint

Mortar joint

Header course of bricks laid across the width of the walll

Closure brick

Foundation of concrete to provide secure base

SETTING OUT A DRY RUN

1 **Set out the** position of the wall with 2 builder's lines a brick's width plus 10mm (½in) apart. Ensure that the lines are equidistant along the length of the proposed wall.

2 **Lay a dry run** of bricks to check for fit, allowing a 10mm- (½in-) space between each. Check the level of the front edge with a spirit level. Chalk the position of the bricks on the foundations.

LAYING THE FIRST STRETCHER COURSE

1 **Throw a mortar** bed 10mm (⅜in) thick and 1 brick wide, along the length of the first course. Furrow with the trowel tip.

2 **Lay the first** brick lengthways on the mortar bed. Check that the brick is level both from end to end and front to back.

3 **Make adjustments** to the level by tapping down gently with the trowel handle. Re-check and do not proceed until it is level.

4 **Set up a builder's line** as a guide to the position for the first course of bricks. Wind the line around a brick at each end to ensure that it remains taut as you work.

5 **Butter the end** face of the next brick, tapering the mortar edges with the trowel to form a 13mm- (⅝in-) thick layer at the centre. This will give a 10mm- (⅜in-) joint.

6 **Working inwards** from either end of the wall, set each brick in its marked position, checking levels as you go. To close the course, butter both end faces of the final brick.

7 **Complete the first course** by laying a row of bricks parallel to the first, checking levels along and across. Fill the collar joint between the rows with mortar.

COMPLETING THE WALL

1 **Throw a mortar bed** on top of the first (stretcher) brick course and lay the next brick course (the header) crossways. Check and adjust the levels as before.

2 **Check the height** of each course with a storey rod and check constantly for levels. To avoid weak joints, if you make a mistake, remove brick and mortar and start again.

3 **Raise up both ends** of the wall by four courses, alternating stretchers and headers. Scrape off excess mortar with the trowel edge as you bed each brick. Neaten joints with a pointing tool.

4 **Once both ends** have been built up, check the levels from end to end, across the wall, and vertically. Check the height of each course with the storey rod.

5 Peg a builder's line into the mortar joint in the built-up end bricks as a guide for the second course. Make sure that it remains taut.

6 Insert a queen closer (*see p.59*) after the first header to maintain staggered joints and avoid having a weak joint running down the wall.

7 As you build, constantly check all levels, horizontal and vertical, and the depth of each course. Move the builder's line up for each new course.

8 Complete the wall with a header course: throw a mortar bed along the length of the wall. Lay the first brick on edge, cross-ways across the wall. Butter one face of each remaining brick and butt it up against the one before. Continue across the length of the wall.

FINISHING THE WALL
To finish the wall and help deflect rainwater, point the mortar joints by running a pointing tool first against the vertical joints, then along the horizontal joints (see also p.69).

CORNERS AND BONDS

Bonding patterns can be both decorative and functional, but not all are equal in structural strength. The stretcher bond is the one most often used for walls that are one brick thick. The English and Flemish bonds are stronger because the header course forms a firm "tie" between the front and back of the wall. Bricks cut in half lengthways (*see p.59*) are used in alternate courses to ensure that joints are staggered. The diagrams below illustrate the laying pattern used for turning corners.

STRETCHER BOND

Staggered stretchers overlap, with the end of one brick at the centre of the one below. Corners are made by alternating stretchers and headers, while half-bats form the final bond at the end of a straight wall.

ENGLISH BOND

In this strong bond for two-brick thick walls, alternate courses of stretchers and headers are laid, with a "queen closer" (a brick cut in half along its length) inserted in header courses to stagger joints.

FLEMISH BOND

An alternative to English bond in a two-brick-thick wall, every course in Flemish bond alternates headers and stretchers. Again, joints are staggered by inserting queen closers after the first header.

Half-bat forms final bond

Queen closer

Queen closer

A BRICK RETAINING WALL

To create low terraces or a raised bed, retaining walls up to 65cm (26in) high can be constructed simply with a single course in stretcher-bond pattern. Large volumes of soil and water exert great pressures and, for anything higher than 65cm (26in), it may be necessary to incorporate reinforcing rods. In this case, seek professional advice.

HINTS & TIPS

• In some places, permission is needed for walls higher than 1m (3ft), and regulations may demand professional construction.
• For extra strength, use concrete blocks and face with bricks for an attractive finish.
• A dry-stone wall (*see p.57*) on a firm foundation can be used for low terraces and forms the ideal niche for many rock plants.

LOW TERRACING
A series of low terraces is a practical self-build proposition and is the ideal way of making a sloping site more accessible. Here, it displays colourful spring bedding plants to perfection.

HOW IT WORKS

A half-brick wall in stretcher bond is built on a concrete footing. A drain (not shown) runs horizontally behind and along the base of the wall, while unmortared vertical joints at every third brick in the lowest course form weep holes: both direct excess water away from the wall. The infill of rubble or gravel assists drainage and helps spread the load. The coping stone deflects rainwater from the wall surface.

A mowing strip, just below soil level, makes a neat edge to the lawn and allows it to be mowed cleanly; it is made from quarter-bats (*see Cutting Bricks, p.59*) laid on mortar.

Coping

Gravel infill

Mowing strip of quarter-bats

Weep hole

Concrete footing

Half-bat completes course

DRY-STONE WALLS

A TRUE DRY-STONE WALL (*see p.57*) is built without mortar and relies on the forces of gravity for its strength and integrity. When the stone used reflects local geology, such walls are unsurpassed for natural effects, especially when planted with rock plants such as sedums or sempervivums. Construction is a satisfying task that demands skill and time; the relatively high cost is merely an accurate reflection of the longevity and durability of the finished article.

MAKING A STONE-EFFECT BLOCK WALL

Some manufacturers offer "dry-stone walling" in kit form. Consistent block size and the use of exterior-grade brick adhesive makes the construction of a realistic facsimile of a dry-stone wall quick and straightforward. The technique does not allow for integral planting pockets but, over time, weathering and colonization by lichens, mosses, and self-seeding wall flora, such as stonecrops (*Sedum*) will enhance the naturalistic effect.

YOU NEED:

TOOLS
• Spade
• Spirit level
• Notched adhesive spreader

MATERIALS
• Hardcore and concrete for footings
• Walling blocks: use standard- (380mm/15in) and two-thirds- (255mm/10in) length blocks for staggered joints
• Quoin-end blocks (i.e. with two adjacent moulded faces): (standard- (380mm/15in) and two-thirds- (255mm/10in) length blocks
• Coping blocks: 380mm (15in) length
• Exterior-grade brick adhesive

LAYING FOOTINGS AND FIRST BLOCK

1 **Construct firm** footings (*see p.47*) 3 times the width of the wall and 300mm (12in) deep: 200mm- (8in-) hardcore layer topped with 100mm- (4in-) concrete layer. Leave the concrete for at least 2 days to cure.

2 **Apply brick adhesive** with a notched adhesive spreader to the lower surface of a two-thirds-length quoin-end block.

3 **Place the block** at one end of the foundations, aligned with the proposed line of the wall. Check the block for levels.

◄ NATURAL HABITAT *Crevices between the stones provide ideal spaces for plants such as sedum.*

BUILDING THE WALL

1 With the first block in place, apply adhesive to a standard-length block. Butt up to the end block; check that the front edges are aligned.

2 Complete the first course, using standard and two-thirds blocks to achieve staggered joints and pressing the blocks firmly together.

3 Start the second course with a standard-length quoin-end block. Check the vertical and horizontal levels as you continue laying blocks.

ADDING THE FINISHING TOUCHES

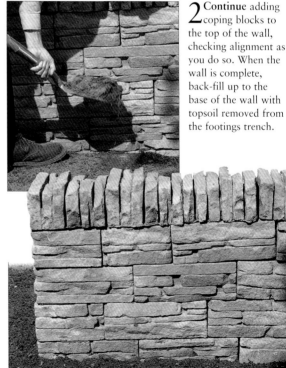

2 Continue adding coping blocks to the top of the wall, checking alignment as you do so. When the wall is complete, back-fill up to the base of the wall with topsoil removed from the footings trench.

1 With the plastic spreader, apply a layer of adhesive to a coping block. Position on top of the finished wall, checking that all outer surfaces are aligned.

THE FINISHED WALL
The wall's pristine appearance will be softened by natural weathering, and can be further enhanced by planting self-clinging climbers in the fertile topsoil at the wall's base.

BUILDING A DRY-STONE WALL

Newly quarried stone is expensive, but stone may be obtained more cheaply as disused quarry waste or reclaimed from derelict walls. For the latter you must obtain permission and check local regulations, as removal of stones may be illegal in protected areas. For a 1m- (3ft-) high wall, you will need about 1 tonne (1 ton) of stone per linear metre (linear yard). Before you begin, you might like to practise your skills on a dry-stone-walling course.

ANATOMY OF A DRY-STONE WALL

Foundation stones are set in a level trench, just below ground level. Every stone touches its neighbour and all joints overlap. Stones are laid level, with the long axis running into the wall, and wedged in with small stones. The gap between the two faces is closely packed as the wall is built. One throughstone per linear metre (linear yard) is inserted halfway up the wall. Copestones are laid from either end towards a central closure, and are wedged in place with V-shaped stones.

SORTING STONES INTO TYPES
Before construction begins, stones are sorted into five basic categories according to their position and function within the wall.

Small filling stones pack the space between the two faces

Throughstones tie faces together at 1m- (3ft-) intervals or less

Building stones decrease in size to give a slope of about 1 in 12

Foundation stones are large, flat, and heavy

Copestones are wedged in place by hammered-in slices of stone

PLANTING IN A DRY-STONE WALL

1 Fill crevice with compost. Place a small rooted cutting (here, sempervivum) on the flat surface of a stone, easing the roots gently into the crevice with a widger.

2 Pack more compost into the crevice to hold the plant securely in position. Firm the plant in with your fingertips, adding more compost if necessary.

3 Once all the plants are in place (here, saxifrages and sempervivum), water from the top of the wall or with a mist spray. Re-firm as needed and keep moist until established.

GETTING DOWN TO BASICS

CHOOSING MATERIALS

THE WEALTH OF WALLING AND FENCING materials on offer can make selection a confusing task, and choice is full of pitfalls for the unwary. Builder's merchants and do-it-yourself suppliers are a prime source of expert advice but, before approaching them, familiarize yourself with commonly available materials and the terms used to describe them, and be clear about what you hope to achieve.

MATERIALS FOR WALLS

Apart from cost and appearance, the most important factors when choosing materials for outdoor use are durability and frost resistance. Clay bricks are graded for "hardiness": for outdoor use they must be frost and moisture resistant if they are not to flake or break in response to freeze–thaw cycles. Do not be tempted to use cheaper, less durable types, and be sure to check the grade if you wish to use recycled bricks.

FROGGED & CORED BRICKS
Filled with mortar, the frog or core helps key in the bricks.

DRY-STONE-EFFECT BLOCKS
Cast in concrete, these blocks are durable and inexpensive.

ROCK-FACED CONCRETE
Finished to look like red bricks or sandstone blocks.

DRESSED STONE BLOCKS
Natural, very expensive, but durable and long lived.

PIERCED CONCRETE BLOCK
Cheap, easy to build, but not structurally strong.

FACING OR STOCK BRICKS
Available in a variety of colours and textures.

CUTTING BRICKS

To cut bricks to size, use a pencil and straightedge to mark a cutting line. Place the brick on a soft surface (here, soft sand). Align bolster chisel with pencil line and strike firmly with a club hammer. Repeat on the opposite face. Place the brick flat and strike again on the pencil line. Repeat each step in turn until the brick breaks.

QUEEN CLOSER AND BATS
Here, a brick is being cut in half lengthways to produce a "queen closer", which is used in a brick wall to maintain staggered joints. A brick cut across its width is known as a "bat".

CONCRETE OR MORTAR?

Mortar and concrete serve different purposes: concrete is used for footings and foundations, while mortar is used to bond brick, stone, or concrete blocks. Both mortar and concrete use cement as the bonding agent.

For concrete footings and foundations, mix 1 part cement, 2½ parts sharp sand, and 3½ parts 10–20mm (½–¾in) aggregate. For masonry mortar, mix 1 part masonry cement with 3 parts soft sand.

Be sure to use the right sand and cement. Soft, or builder's, sand is fine grade and salt free; sharp sand is coarser. Masonry cement is a ready-made mix with additives designed to lend greater workability.

USEFUL TERMS

Cement: a grey powder containing limestone, that reacts chemically to form a bonding agent when mixed with water.
Concrete: a mix of cement, sharp sand, coarse aggregate, and water.
Mortar: a mix of cement, sand, and water.

MIXING MASONRY MORTAR

1 Place measured quantities of dry, soft sand and cement on a suitable flat surface. Mix together thoroughly with a shovel.

2 Make a well in the pile of sand and cement and add a little clean tap water. Blend it in with a shovel, adding more water as necessary.

3 Mix until smooth and firm, and furrows made with a shovel hold their shape. If too wet, mortar will run; if too dry, joints will be weak.

DIFFERENT TYPES OF FENCING

The choice of fence is dictated first by its intended function and then by aesthetics. If security and privacy are priorities, choose closeboard, waney-edged panel, or interference fencing. Pickets make a good-looking boundary, but offer little security and no privacy. Ranch-style (planed boards attached horizontally to stout posts) and post-and-rail fencing (horizontal poles or rough-sawn timber between posts) are similarly insecure but form a low-cost boundary. Chestnut paling is, at best, a temporary measure, while post-and-wire variants play a valuable stockproofing role. Both are best camouflaged by plantings.

LIFE EXPECTANCY

• Timber that has been pressure treated with preservative is best for outdoor use. If cut on site, be sure to treat all cut surfaces.

• Timber varies in durability. Oak, larch, sweet chestnut, and western red cedar have a life of 10–25 years if untreated; ash, Scots pine, spruce, and Douglas fir last 5–10 years if untreated, extending to 10–25 years with preservative treatment.

• Chainlink or welded galvanized wire last 10 years, more if the wire is plastic coated.

• Very expensive tropical timbers, like iroko, last a lifetime, but do check that they come from sustainable forestry sources.

WOOD IN VARIETY
From top: picket fence, post-and-rail, chestnut paling, ranch-style fencing.

VARIATIONS ON POST-AND-WIRE
From top: chainlink fencing and welded wire are both stockproof, but more functional than pretty; post-and-chain provides an inexpensive boundary.

▼TRELLIS
Available in planed hardwood (costly, but sturdiest for screens), or less durable sawn softwood.

►INTERFERENCE FENCING
Horizontal boards, alternating on either side of posts, are an efficient wind filter.

Supporting Posts

A fence is only as strong as its supporting posts and, for strength and durability, concrete wins hands down. Concrete outlasts any timber and is maintenance free, even below ground, because it resists the destructive action of ground water. Grooved concrete posts offer an easy fixing for panel fences but, if a less utilitarian appearance is desired, you can use concrete spurs (*right*), which are pre-drilled for easy fixing of timber posts.

Pressure-treated timber posts come twice-weathered (shaped to a point) or flat, to take a decorative weather cap. Pressure-treated rustic poles are available for post-and-rail or rustic-work fences. Even treated timber rots eventually in contact with wet soil and, although an additional coat of preservative prolongs their life, wooden posts that touch damp soil will still need to be replaced within 10–15 years.

Grooved concrete post

Tall concrete spur

Timber post

Treated rustic pole

FENCE POSTS
A range of fence posts, of varying durability and cost, is available but, when considering price, take into account the time and expense of subsequent maintenance treatments.

Choosing Timber

Although both desirable and suitable for outdoor use, some hardwoods, such as oak, are very expensive. Softwoods, like larch and western red cedar, are less costly. All three are long lived without preservative. Most other softwoods are even less expensive, but must be preservative treated. Pressure treatment forces preservative deep into the wood and gives a much longer life than a simple surface coating.

Timber for outdoor use is often described as durable, as distinct from non-durable woods for indoor use. Timber merchants offer timber rough sawn or planed, and will often cut to length. Sawn timber is usually cheapest and fine for most fencing, but choose planed timber if you wish to apply a wood paint to the finished fence.

PLANED-ALL-ROUND (PAR) TIMBER
Planed boards have a smooth surface that is ideal for a crisply painted finish.

ROUGH-SAWN TIMBER
This is adequate for most fencing purposes and can be stained to colour the wood.

SURFACE-TREATED TIMBER
A surface treatment of preservative is effective but needs to be re-applied regularly.

TOOLS FOR THE JOB

WHATEVER THE TASK IN HAND, it is invariably made easier by using the correct tools for the job. Simple items, such as a straightedge, levelling pegs, or storey rod (*see p.50*), can be made at home from timber offcuts. Many small tools, such as pointing trowels, are unlikely to be used frequently, so quality and durability are less important to you than to a professional; in these cases, you can keep outlay down by choosing the cheapest tools in the range.

INVESTING IN TOOLS

For some jobs, high-quality tools really do contribute to achieving a professional finish. For building work, in particular, accurate measurement and levelling are the key to producing safe structures, so buying the best tools that you can afford is easily justified. Good measuring tools will come in useful for many other projects about the home and garden and, if you keep them clean and take good care of them, they will last a lifetime.

Builder's square

LEVEL AND SQUARE
Clockwise from top left are builder's square, tape, pegs, straightedge, spirit level.

TOOLS FOR WALLS

Brick and stonework need several specialist tools: those shown below are the minimum you need to own, buy, or borrow.

The sturdiest (and most expensive) trowels are cast from a single piece of steel. Those with welded handles often break with prolonged use, but are much cheaper and perfectly adequate for one-off jobs.

You may also need a line level, and a soft, long-bristled brush is handy for cleaning surfaces before applying mortar.

CARE OF TOOLS

• Immediately after use, wash in clean water all tools that come into contact with cement or mortar. Both set hard and are difficult to remove if left to dry.

• Keep metal parts sound and rust free by washing, drying, and wiping with an oily rag after use. Store tools in a dry, airy place.

• Wooden handles last longer if wiped over occasionally with linseed oil.

BRICK TROWEL

Available in different shapes for different pointing patterns

CLUB HAMMER

Blade width varies from 75–100mm (3–4in): the wider the better

String of non-shrink polypropylene for accurate lining out

POINTING TOOL

BOLSTER CHISEL

POINTING TROWEL

BUILDER'S LINE

TOOLS FOR FENCES

You may find that most tools needed for fence construction are already part of your home toolkit but, if you do need to buy, the following are most useful.

A crosscut saw, which is designed to cut timber across the grain (rip-saws cut along the grain and a general purpose saw does both). The easiest way to cut fancy shapes is with a jigsaw attachment on a power drill; if you have to do it by hand, use a fret saw or coping saw.

A chisel and wooden-headed mallet are used for cutting slot or mortise joints. Mortise chisels have handles that are reinforced to take punishment from the mallet; a bevel-edge chisel is similar but, being slightly broader, is easier and quicker for the amateur to use.

CLAW HAMMER

CHISEL

The more points per centimetre (inch), the finer the finished cut surface

CROSSCUT SAW

Round and oval wire nails are cheapest bought by weight

GALVANIZED NAILS

SAFE USE OF POWER TOOLS

• Always fit an RCD (residual current device or circuit breaker) when using power tools outdoors.
• Never use electrical tools during or just after rain.
• Use earthed extension cables with the same number of wires as the tool.
• Disconnect power before adjusting, inspecting, or cleaning an electrical tool.

HIRING SPECIALIST EQUIPMENT

Good specialist hire companies carry an extensive range of tools and machinery, so it is always worth checking what is on offer before buying tools that you may use only once. They will also advise on the most suitable equipment for the job in hand. Hiring can be for a full or half day.

Digging post holes and mixing concrete or mortar, in particular, require strength and fitness. A manual post-hole borer or auger is helpful for extensive runs of fencing, and a concrete mixer saves a good deal of effort when laying footings.

It is essential, especially if you are not used to operating machinery, that you get a demonstration of how equipment works and how to use it safely. Before accepting delivery of any hired items, check that everything looks well maintained and that equipment is running smoothly.

CHECKLIST

• Check the condition and smooth running of equipment before accepting delivery.
• Ask for a demonstration and ensure that you know how to operate all machinery safely. Don't forget to check on fuel requirements for motorized machines.
• Make sure that you wear any appropriate safety gear; you may be able to hire goggles and ear defenders.
• When using concrete mixers, wear close-fitting clothing and stout gloves and boots. Keep your head, hands, and shovels clear of moving parts.
• Make all possible preparations, such as lining out and trench digging, before taking delivery of hired equipment.
• Do not underestimate how long you will need the hired equipment for: you may be charged a higher rate for additional days.

PREPARING FOR ACTION

B Y THE TIME YOU ARE READY TO BUILD, you will have made sure that your skills
are adequate for safe completion of the project, and that the project
conforms with any legal and building regulation requirements. Accurately work
out overall dimensions in readiness for estimating and ordering materials. Plan
ahead for taking delivery, giving consideration to site access and storage of
materials. If necessary, recruit a team of helpers to move heavy items.

ORDERING AND DELIVERY

Calculating quantities is a daunting task
for the beginner, but a reputable builder's
merchant or do-it-yourself supplier will
be happy to advise if given accurate
dimensions for the task in hand.

Ask about the supplier's sale or return
policy: many accept returns of unopened
bagged materials. Check transport and
delivery arrangements, and be on hand to
ensure that delivery is made as near to the
site as possible to minimize the heavy
labour of transporting materials later.

Have ready wooden pallets and plastic
sheeting to provide dry, off-ground storage
of bricks and cement.

ESTIMATING QUANTITIES

• When estimating quantities, work in either
metric or imperial measurements: do not mix
the two.
• Area equals length x width.
• Volume equals length x width x depth.
• For a half-brick wall, you will need 60
bricks per square metre (50 per square yard);
120 (100) for a full-brick wall. You will need
10–12 concrete walling blocks per square
metre (8–10 per square yard). Allow 5–10%
for wastage.
• Calculate concrete and its constituents by
volume in cubic metres (cubic yards).

A GLOSSARY OF USEFUL TERMS

Aggregate: crushed stone or gravel (usually
10–20mm- (½–¾in-) grade) used in making
concrete.
Bat: a piece of a whole brick. A half-bat is a
brick cut in half across its width; a quarter-bat
is half the length of a half-bat.
Bed: a horizontal layer of mortar on which
bricks are laid.
Bond: the arrangement of bricks in a wall
(bond pattern, *see p.52*), or the area of
adhesion between masonry units.
Buttering: applying mortar to a brick face.
Closer: the final brick that closes a course. A
brick cut in half along its length is sometimes
called a queen closer.
Coping: protective cap, often made of pre-cast
concrete, laid on top of a wall to shed water.
Course: a layer of bricks in a structure. Bricks
in the **header** course lie across the wall;
stretchers line up along the length of wall.

Face: the exposed surface of a brick.
Footing: the concrete layer of a foundation.
Foundation: the below-ground structural
support for a structure.
Hardcore: rubble, when used as a sub-base for
concrete footings.
Header: *see* **Course**
Joint: the layer of mortar between bricks,
usually a standard 10mm (½in). Cross joints
are vertical joints; bed joints are horizontal.
Collar joints link two sides of a wall together.
Lead: 3–4 courses of bricks built up at the ends
of a wall before building the body of the wall.
Pointing: the surface finish of a mortar joint.
Stretcher: *see* **Course**
Throwing: the act of applying mortar to a bed.
Twice-weathered: (of timber or concrete
copings) shaped to a point with two sides.
Weep hole: a vertical gap left between two
bricks to allow for drainage.

BUILDING AND PLANNING REGULATIONS

Much building and planning legislation is framed primarily with public safety in mind. For example, the height restrictions on walls and fences are designed to prevent the obstruction of clear visibility on public highways. The panel below contains an outline of the law as applied to walls and fences – but it must be emphasized, if you have any doubts at all, for the safety of yourself and others, seek expert advice.

PLANNING REGULATIONS ON WALLS AND FENCES

• If a wall or fence lies on a boundary between two properties, or fronts onto a highway or public thoroughfare, it must lie on your side of the boundary. It is always prudent and polite to consult your neighbours before constructing walls or fences.

• The height of any gate, wall, or fence adjacent to a highway used by vehicular traffic must not exceed 1m (3ft) above ground level. The height of any other gate, wall, or fence must not exceed 2m (6ft) above ground level. These are permitted minor operations; anything taller will need planning permission.

• In many places, retaining walls in excess of 1m (3ft) in height are governed by building regulations. Anything more than 1.2m (4ft) is a job for a professional; if higher than 2.4m (8ft), this means an architect or engineer.

• Consultation: if you are at all unsure about your project, it is advisable to consult your local authority's building or planning control department to check whether planning permission is needed for a wall or fence, especially if your home is a listed building or in a conservation area where special restrictions may apply. Your local building and planning control officers are the experts; seek their help before rather than after the event. Remember that they are empowered to make you remove structures that contravene the law.

PRECAUTIONS AND SAFETY

Garden and do-it-yourself accidents acount for a major proportion of home-based incidents, and the potential for serious injury increases when using heavy machinery and electrical tools. Ensure that powered equipment is in good order and that you know how to use it. Wear stout gloves to keep mortar and cement off your skin; in the event of contact, wash in copious amounts of clean water to avoid burns. Protect your eyes with goggles whenever you cut brick or stone.

PROTECTIVE
GLOVES

SAFETY GOGGLES

INCORRECT POSTURE   CORRECT POSTURE

PROTECT YOUR BACK
Never lift by bending from the waist: use the strength of your legs – not your lumbar region – to lift the load. Don't attempt to twist and lift at the same time: you can injure your back by reaching and lifting even relatively light weights. Always carry heavy weights close to your body, and use a barrow or trolley whenever possible. Don't overestimate your strength.

LEVEL AND TRUE

The safety and stability of any structure depends on all corners being square, all lines being straight, and every surface being level in three directions: along its length, across its width, and vertically. Check these three levels constantly during construction.

To find a true corner, mark the line of a wall with two pegs, one at either end. Measure 40cm (16in) along the line beyond the desired position of the corner. Place a second peg, by eye, at right angles to the line, 30cm (12in) away from the corner, and then adjust its position until the diagonal line between the two pegs measures 50cm (20in). The corner opposite the 50cm (20in) side of a triangle so constructed is a perfect right angle, as are all four angles around the corner point (*see illustration right*).

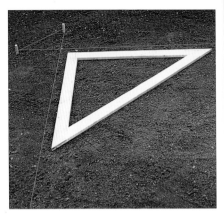

MARKING OUT A TRUE CORNER
Use simple geometry to create a corner: all triangles with sides in the proportions 3:4:5 form a right-angled corner opposite the longest side. Check with a builder's square.

THE IMPORTANCE OF FOUNDATIONS

A wall is only as strong as its foundations, whose dimensions are calculated according to the size of the wall, the method of construction, and soil type and condition.

Most walls up to 65cm (26in) high do not need substantial foundations. Those 65–100cm (26–39in) in height need a concrete foundation two to three times the width of the wall, with a depth at least equal to the wall's width. The footing must have a level surface, with straight and true sides. As its base must be on firm subsoil,

the depth may have to be increased. In areas with severe winters, footings must be deeper so that they are below the frostline.

Half-brick walls should be no higher than 65cm (26in) and, if higher than 45cm (18in), they must have supporting piers at 3m- (10ft-) intervals. Full-brick walls higher than 65cm (26in) must be built with a bond that ties the wall together.

For walls over 1m (3ft) in height, especially those on clay or silt soils, it is advisable to seek professional advice.

GUIDELINE DIMENSIONS FOR SELF-BUILD WALLS

TYPE OF WALL	WALL HEIGHT	FOOTING DEPTH	FOOTING WIDTH
• **Half-brick wall** 102mm (4in) thick	• 45–65cm (18–26in)	• 110–150mm (4½–6in)	• 205–300mm (8–12in)
• **Piers** for half-brick wall	• 45–65cm (18–26in)	• 460–610mm (18–24in)	• 460–610mm, (18–24in)
• **Full-brick wall** 215mm (8in) thick	• Up to 1m (3ft)	• 230–300mm (9–12in)	• 450–600mm (18–24in)

LOOKING AFTER YOUR STRUCTURES

All structures, whether of timber, brick, or stone, need a degree of maintenance to protect the investment of time, effort, and money that they represent. For brick and stonework, only low-level, infrequent maintenance is required, but timber is more demanding. Pressure-treated and naturally durable timbers, like oak and cedar, need only occasional applications of additional preservatives, while less durable and untreated wood require more regular treatment.

PRESERVING WOOD

Preservatives come in several forms and in a range of colours: apply creosote and water-based types every four years, those based on solvent every two to three years. Creosote is toxic to plants, and poisonous if swallowed, inhaled, or absorbed via the skin, so solvent-based types are usually preferable. As the range is confusingly wide, check with the supplier that the one you have chosen suits the particular job.

GO WITH THE GRAIN
Always apply timber treatments to clean, dry, dust-free surfaces and paint along the grain of the wood. Test the colour on a small area, first, to check the effect.

THE RIGHT FINISH

There are two basic methods of colouring wood: with paint or with stain. Wood stains darken and/or colour the wood but, being translucent, they still allow the beauty of the grain to show through. Many exterior-grade wood stains also include preservative; they are prepared in a water, solvent, or oil base. In general, the latter are the easiest to apply as they dry slowly.

Exterior wood paints are acrylics, specially formulated to give a finish that allows the timber to "breathe", thus reducing flaking and cracking. For a long-lasting finish, apply over coats of wood primer and undercoat. To achieve a smooth finish on planed timber, rub off rough spots and edges with sandpaper, then wipe over with white spirit to remove any dust.

HINTS AND TIPS

- Make sure that all freshly cut timber surfaces are treated with preservative, even when using pressure-treated timber.
- Keep all preservatives, especially creosote, away from plants and off your skin by wearing protective gloves and clothing.
- Apply paints, stains, and preservatives to dry, clean, dust-free timber. Always work along the grain with a good-quality brush that will not shed its bristles as you work.
- Use only exterior-grade wood paints outdoors and don't forget the end grain. Using a primer and undercoat made by the same manufacturer guarantees compatibility.
- For all surface finishes, always read the label advice with regard to number of coats needed, drying time, and coverage.

REPLACING ROTTEN POSTS

Concrete spurs have a clear advantage when it comes to post replacement; simply unbolt the old post and bolt the new one in place. You may be able to lift and replace posts set in concrete if the footing is sound, filling any gaps with instant cement to avoid water penetration. If not, you will have to dig out and renew both post and foundation.

Damaged post
Stone
Timber offcut

REMOVING A ROTTEN POST
Lash a timber offcut to the bottom of the rotten post as near to the ground as possible. Using a large stone as a pivot, apply downward pressure to lever out the the post.

Galvanized bolt
Nail
Concrete spur
Fence post

Wooden support
Fence post
Concrete
Hardcore

REPLACING A POST ON A CONCRETE SPUR
Drive two nails into the damaged post and take the weight of the post by bracing, as shown, before unbolting. Mark and pre-drill bolt holes in the new post before replacing.

REPLACING A WOODEN POST
Detach panels; dig out post and foundations. Renew post and foundation (see p.31–32). Brace the new post vertically and leave in place for a week until the concrete has cured.

WIRE PLANT SUPPORTS FOR FENCES

Attach horizontal or vertical wires to vine eyes screwed into the support posts. To avoid sagging, tauten the wires by tightening the vine eyes with pliers or by using tensioners. Space wires 30–45cm (12–18in) apart, with the lowest 30cm (12in) above soil level.

Vine eye

USING VINE EYES
Allow a minimum 5cm (2in) clearance between fence and wire to permit adequate air circulation and reduce the risk of fungal diseases.

REPOINTING BRICKWORK

Well-built walls may not need attention for 10–15 years, but any repointing should be done as soon as it is necessary. Remove old mortar with a cold chisel and club hammer to a depth of 2cm (¾in). Mist joints with a fine water spray and repoint. Cover with a plastic sheet for about four days to ensure the slow cure needed for strong joints.

PROS AND CONS

• V-shaped birdsmouth, recessed weather-struck, or half-round patterns shed water well and are the most durable for outdoor use.
• Rubbed and flush pointings shed water moderately well and are acceptably durable outdoors if used with a concrete coping.

| BIRDSMOUTH | WEATHER-STRUCK | HALF-ROUND | RUBBED | FLUSH |

PAINTING WALLS

A stucco-rendered surface (coated in a mix of one part cement to three to five parts fine sand) gives the finest surface for painting, but even regular brickwork can be given a coat of colour provided you use paints that are formulated for outdoor use.

Prepare surfaces thoroughly so that they are clean and dust free, and deal with any small cracks before painting. Check and follow manufacturer's recommendations for priming requirements as these vary according to formulation.

PAINTS FOR WALLS

Exterior emulsion paint is available in a wide range of colours and, although water based, is surprisingly durable for outdoor use. Apply to sound, clean surfaces with a good-quality brush or roller.
Masonry paint is an exceptionally hard-wearing finish for rendered surfaces as it usually contains silica or nylon additives for strong cohesion. Surfaces usually need priming with stabilizers; fungicides may also be recommended to reduce staining.

ATTACHING TRELLIS TO A WALL

The simplest method is to screw trellis panels onto a framework of vertical, 5cm-(2in-) thick wooden battens. A hooked and hinged fixing allows access to the wall for maintenance: attach horizontal battens to both wall and trellis panel, with two hinges at the bottom and hooks and vine eyes on both sides at the top.

BATTEN FIXING
Using galvanized screws, fix vertical battens, at least 5cm-(2in-) thick, to the wall.

BOTTOM-HINGED
Two sturdy hinges attached to horizontal battens allow a trellis panel to be lowered.

TOP HOOKS
A hook and vine eye on both sides of the batten hold the trellis panel in place.

INDEX

ACKNOWLEDGMENTS

Picture research Cathie Arrington
Special photography Peter Anderson and Steve Gorton
Illustrations Vanessa Luff
Additional illustrations Karen Gavin
Index Hilary Bird

Dorling Kindersley would like to thank:
Denise O'Brien and Neale Chamberlain for sourcing pictures from the DK library; Marshalls for generously providing advice and materials for the stone-effect block wall; John Murphy for his bricklaying skills; and all staff at the RHS, in particular Susanne Mitchell, Karen Wilson and Barbara Haynes at Vincent Square and Nick Freed at Wisley.

The Royal Horticultural Society
To learn more about the work of the society, visit the RHS on the Internet at www.rhs.org.uk. Information includes news of events around the country, a horticultural database, international plant registers, results of plant trials, and membership details.

Photography
The publisher would also like to thank the following for their kind permission to reproduce their photographs:

(key: t=top, c=centre, b=below, l=left, r=right, fc=front cover, bc=back cover)

Garden Picture Library: John Baker 8; Mark Bolton 23t; Rex Butcher 16t, Brian Carter 19t, 53c; Vaughan Fleming 19bl; Jacqui Hurst 15b; Ann Kelly 22t; Lamontagne 17b; Jerry Pavia 9t, 13tl, 13b; Gary Rogers 4bl, 41b; J.S. Sira 46; Janet Sorrell 2, 20b; Ron Sutherland 5bl, 7, 11r, 14b, 16b, 17tl; Nigel Temple 54; Brigitte Thomas 13tr, 14t, 26l; Mel Watson 18
John Glover Photography: 20t, 21
Harpur Garden Library: 42
Clive Nichols Garden Pictures:
L. Hampden/J & C Nichols 5br, 10; Leeds City Council – Chelsea 1998 4br, 15t, 22c; Andrew & Karla Newell 23b
Photos Horticultural: 6, 9b, 11l, 12c, 12b, 17tr, 19br, 24, 25, 27, 28r, 29, 30, 36

Jacket: commissioned photography with the exception of **Garden Picture Library:** Rex Butcher fc bl; Vaughan Fleming fc tl; Jerry Pavia bc tl; Ron Sutherland bc flap; Mel Watson fc flap;
John Glover: fc cl;
Clive Nichols Garden Pictures: Leeds City Council – Chelsea 1998 bc b, bc tr